FAMILY TREE

NOTEBOOK

POCKET
Edition

"Know from whence you came. If you know whence you came, there are absolutely no limitations to where you can go." - James Baldwin

Table of Contents

How to Use this Book

- Use the <u>Quick Index by Ancestor</u> to write down the names of your family members and the pages where you can find them. Then it's just a quick flick to find what you wrote about any of your ancestors up to the 6th generation.

- If you join any genealogy websites or online archives, use the <u>Membership</u> tables to keep track of your passwords and how long you have access to them for.

- <u>Important Contacts</u> is a space for you to jot down the contact details of any hired researchers or other important collaborators.

- <u>Pedigree Charts and Notes</u> – The core of your research. There are two lineage charts: one for your paternal ancestors and one for your maternal ancestors.

- On the page following each lineage chart, you will find a dedicated space for <u>Alternative Information</u> and other <u>Notes</u>.

- In the <u>Ancestor Data Sheets</u> you will be able to record all relevant information for each of your ancestors up to the 6th generation (62 sheets).

- The <u>To-Do List</u> is somewhere you can write down all pending tasks or ideas for future research.

- <u>Tips and Ideas</u> is there just in case you get stuck in your research. We have all had those moments that we don't know how to keep going and we just need someone to tell us something different to help us discover new paths to explore. Based on my 15-years experience researching my family across 10 countries, I have put together a concise list for beginners, intermediates and more advanced researchers, to help spark new ideas to avoid getting bogged down.

- You can use the <u>Archive Log</u> to write down all relevant information you find when you visit an archive or an online source.

- <u>DNA Results Log</u> is the place for you to record the results of any test you or your relatives have taken.

- During your research journey, you're sure to start discovering new stories or anecdotes that will give life to the people who were previously just names and dates on your tree. <u>Stories to Remember</u> is the perfect place for you to write these down.

Quick Index by Ancestor

Relative's Name	Pages	Relative's Name	Pages

Relative's Name	Pages	Relative's Name	Pages

Memberships

Name	
Website / Address	
Start date	
End date	
Cost	
Username	
Password	

Name	
Website / Address	
Start date	
End date	
Cost	
Username	
Password	

Important Contacts

Name	
Position	
City / Country	
Phone	
Email	
Website / Address	
Comments	

Name	
Position	
City / Country	
Phone	
Email	
Website / Address	
Comments	

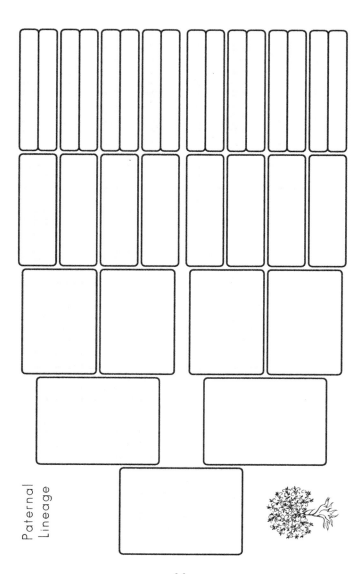

Paternal
Lineage

Alternative Information
Spellings, Dates of Birth, Places of Death, etc.

_____

_____

_____

_____

_____

_____

Other Notes

_____

_____

_____

_____

_____

_____

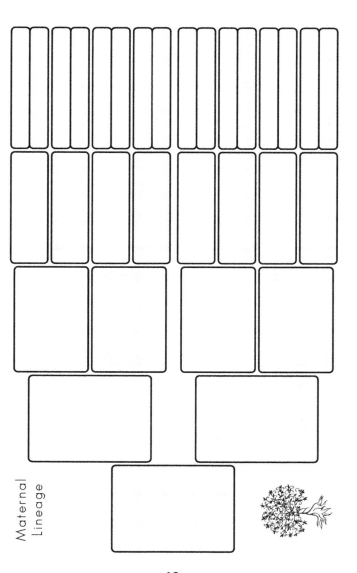

Maternal Lineage

Alternative Information
Spellings, Dates of Birth, Places of Death, etc.

_____

_____

_____

_____

_____

_____

Other Notes

_____

_____

_____

_____

_____

_____

Ancestor Data Sheets

Name	
Alternative Spellings	
Date and Place of Birth	
Date and Place of Marriage	
Date and Place of Death	
Parents	
Spouse	
Children	
Comments *Profession, Personality, Nationalities, Other spouses, Religion, Education, Siblings, Sponsors, Distinctive features, Languages spoken, Health conditions, Passport number, Life events, etc.*	

Name	
Alternative Spellings	
Date and Place of Birth	
Date and Place of Marriage	
Date and Place of Death	
Parents	
Spouse	
Children	
Comments *Profession, Personality, Nationalities, Other spouses, Religion, Education, Siblings, Sponsors, Distinctive features, Languages spoken, Health conditions, Passport number, Life events, etc.*	

Name	
Alternative Spellings	
Date and Place of Birth	
Date and Place of Marriage	
Date and Place of Death	
Parents	
Spouse	
Children	
Comments *Profession,* *Personality,* *Nationalities,* *Other spouses,* *Religion,* *Education,* *Siblings, Sponsors,* *Distinctive* *features,* *Languages spoken,* *Health conditions,* *Passport number,* *Life events, etc.*	

Name	
Alternative Spellings	
Date and Place of Birth	
Date and Place of Marriage	
Date and Place of Death	
Parents	
Spouse	
Children	
Comments *Profession, Personality, Nationalities, Other spouses, Religion, Education, Siblings, Sponsors, Distinctive features, Languages spoken, Health conditions, Passport number, Life events, etc.*	

Name	
Alternative Spellings	
Date and Place of Birth	
Date and Place of Marriage	
Date and Place of Death	
Parents	
Spouse	
Children	
Comments *Profession,* *Personality,* *Nationalities,* *Other spouses,* *Religion,* *Education,* *Siblings, Sponsors,* *Distinctive* *features,* *Languages spoken,* *Health conditions,* *Passport number,* *Life events, etc.*	

Name	
Alternative Spellings	
Date and Place of Birth	
Date and Place of Marriage	
Date and Place of Death	
Parents	
Spouse	
Children	
Comments *Profession, Personality, Nationalities, Other spouses, Religion, Education, Siblings, Sponsors, Distinctive features, Languages spoken, Health conditions, Passport number, Life events, etc.*	

Name	
Alternative Spellings	
Date and Place of Birth	
Date and Place of Marriage	
Date and Place of Death	
Parents	
Spouse	
Children	
Comments *Profession, Personality, Nationalities, Other spouses, Religion, Education, Siblings, Sponsors, Distinctive features, Languages spoken, Health conditions, Passport number, Life events, etc.*	

Name	
Alternative Spellings	
Date and Place of Birth	
Date and Place of Marriage	
Date and Place of Death	
Parents	
Spouse	
Children	
Comments *Profession, Personality, Nationalities, Other spouses, Religion, Education, Siblings, Sponsors, Distinctive features, Languages spoken, Health conditions, Passport number, Life events, etc.*	

Name	
Alternative Spellings	
Date and Place of Birth	
Date and Place of Marriage	
Date and Place of Death	
Parents	
Spouse	
Children	
Comments *Profession, Personality, Nationalities, Other spouses, Religion, Education, Siblings, Sponsors, Distinctive features, Languages spoken, Health conditions, Passport number, Life events, etc.*	

Name	
Alternative Spellings	
Date and Place of Birth	
Date and Place of Marriage	
Date and Place of Death	
Parents	
Spouse	
Children	
Comments *Profession, Personality, Nationalities, Other spouses, Religion, Education, Siblings, Sponsors, Distinctive features, Languages spoken, Health conditions, Passport number, Life events, etc.*	

Name	
Alternative Spellings	
Date and Place of Birth	
Date and Place of Marriage	
Date and Place of Death	
Parents	
Spouse	
Children	
Comments *Profession, Personality, Nationalities, Other spouses, Religion, Education, Siblings, Sponsors, Distinctive features, Languages spoken, Health conditions, Passport number, Life events, etc.*	

Name	
Alternative Spellings	
Date and Place of Birth	
Date and Place of Marriage	
Date and Place of Death	
Parents	
Spouse	
Children	
Comments *Profession, Personality, Nationalities, Other spouses, Religion, Education, Siblings, Sponsors, Distinctive features, Languages spoken, Health conditions, Passport number, Life events, etc.*	

Name	
Alternative Spellings	
Date and Place of Birth	
Date and Place of Marriage	
Date and Place of Death	
Parents	
Spouse	
Children	
Comments *Profession, Personality, Nationalities, Other spouses, Religion, Education, Siblings, Sponsors, Distinctive features, Languages spoken, Health conditions, Passport number, Life events, etc.*	

Name	
Alternative Spellings	
Date and Place of Birth	
Date and Place of Marriage	
Date and Place of Death	
Parents	
Spouse	
Children	
Comments *Profession, Personality, Nationalities, Other spouses, Religion, Education, Siblings, Sponsors, Distinctive features, Languages spoken, Health conditions, Passport number, Life events, etc.*	

Name	
Alternative Spellings	
Date and Place of Birth	
Date and Place of Marriage	
Date and Place of Death	
Parents	
Spouse	
Children	
Comments *Profession, Personality, Nationalities, Other spouses, Religion, Education, Siblings, Sponsors, Distinctive features, Languages spoken, Health conditions, Passport number, Life events, etc.*	

Name	
Alternative Spellings	
Date and Place of Birth	
Date and Place of Marriage	
Date and Place of Death	
Parents	
Spouse	
Children	
Comments *Profession, Personality, Nationalities, Other spouses, Religion, Education, Siblings, Sponsors, Distinctive features, Languages spoken, Health conditions, Passport number, Life events, etc.*	

Name	
Alternative Spellings	
Date and Place of Birth	
Date and Place of Marriage	
Date and Place of Death	
Parents	
Spouse	
Children	
Comments *Profession, Personality, Nationalities, Other spouses, Religion, Education, Siblings, Sponsors, Distinctive features, Languages spoken, Health conditions, Passport number, Life events, etc.*	

Name	
Alternative Spellings	
Date and Place of Birth	
Date and Place of Marriage	
Date and Place of Death	
Parents	
Spouse	
Children	
Comments *Profession, Personality, Nationalities, Other spouses, Religion, Education, Siblings, Sponsors, Distinctive features, Languages spoken, Health conditions, Passport number, Life events, etc.*	

Name	
Alternative Spellings	
Date and Place of Birth	
Date and Place of Marriage	
Date and Place of Death	
Parents	
Spouse	
Children	
Comments *Profession, Personality, Nationalities, Other spouses, Religion, Education, Siblings, Sponsors, Distinctive features, Languages spoken, Health conditions, Passport number, Life events, etc.*	

Name	
Alternative Spellings	
Date and Place of Birth	
Date and Place of Marriage	
Date and Place of Death	
Parents	
Spouse	
Children	
Comments *Profession, Personality, Nationalities, Other spouses, Religion, Education, Siblings, Sponsors, Distinctive features, Languages spoken, Health conditions, Passport number, Life events, etc.*	

Name	
Alternative Spellings	
Date and Place of Birth	
Date and Place of Marriage	
Date and Place of Death	
Parents	
Spouse	
Children	
Comments *Profession, Personality, Nationalities, Other spouses, Religion, Education, Siblings, Sponsors, Distinctive features, Languages spoken, Health conditions, Passport number, Life events, etc.*	

Name	
Alternative Spellings	
Date and Place of Birth	
Date and Place of Marriage	
Date and Place of Death	
Parents	
Spouse	
Children	
Comments *Profession, Personality, Nationalities, Other spouses, Religion, Education, Siblings, Sponsors, Distinctive features, Languages spoken, Health conditions, Passport number, Life events, etc.*	

Name	
Alternative Spellings	
Date and Place of Birth	
Date and Place of Marriage	
Date and Place of Death	
Parents	
Spouse	
Children	
Comments *Profession, Personality, Nationalities, Other spouses, Religion, Education, Siblings, Sponsors, Distinctive features, Languages spoken, Health conditions, Passport number, Life events, etc.*	

Name	
Alternative Spellings	
Date and Place of Birth	
Date and Place of Marriage	
Date and Place of Death	
Parents	
Spouse	
Children	
Comments *Profession, Personality, Nationalities, Other spouses, Religion, Education, Siblings, Sponsors, Distinctive features, Languages spoken, Health conditions, Passport number, Life events, etc.*	

Name	
Alternative Spellings	
Date and Place of Birth	
Date and Place of Marriage	
Date and Place of Death	
Parents	
Spouse	
Children	
Comments *Profession, Personality, Nationalities, Other spouses, Religion, Education, Siblings, Sponsors, Distinctive features, Languages spoken, Health conditions, Passport number, Life events, etc.*	

Name	
Alternative Spellings	
Date and Place of Birth	
Date and Place of Marriage	
Date and Place of Death	
Parents	
Spouse	
Children	
Comments *Profession, Personality, Nationalities, Other spouses, Religion, Education, Siblings, Sponsors, Distinctive features, Languages spoken, Health conditions, Passport number, Life events, etc.*	

Name	
Alternative Spellings	
Date and Place of Birth	
Date and Place of Marriage	
Date and Place of Death	
Parents	
Spouse	
Children	
Comments *Profession, Personality, Nationalities, Other spouses, Religion, Education, Siblings, Sponsors, Distinctive features, Languages spoken, Health conditions, Passport number, Life events, etc.*	

Name	
Alternative Spellings	
Date and Place of Birth	
Date and Place of Marriage	
Date and Place of Death	
Parents	
Spouse	
Children	
Comments *Profession,* *Personality,* *Nationalities,* *Other spouses,* *Religion,* *Education,* *Siblings, Sponsors,* *Distinctive* *features,* *Languages spoken,* *Health conditions,* *Passport number,* *Life events, etc.*	

Name	
Alternative Spellings	
Date and Place of Birth	
Date and Place of Marriage	
Date and Place of Death	
Parents	
Spouse	
Children	
Comments *Profession, Personality, Nationalities, Other spouses, Religion, Education, Siblings, Sponsors, Distinctive features, Languages spoken, Health conditions, Passport number, Life events, etc.*	

Name	
Alternative Spellings	
Date and Place of Birth	
Date and Place of Marriage	
Date and Place of Death	
Parents	
Spouse	
Children	
Comments *Profession, Personality, Nationalities, Other spouses, Religion, Education, Siblings, Sponsors, Distinctive features, Languages spoken, Health conditions, Passport number, Life events, etc.*	

Name	
Alternative Spellings	
Date and Place of Birth	
Date and Place of Marriage	
Date and Place of Death	
Parents	
Spouse	
Children	
Comments *Profession,* *Personality,* *Nationalities,* *Other spouses,* *Religion,* *Education,* *Siblings, Sponsors,* *Distinctive* *features,* *Languages spoken,* *Health conditions,* *Passport number,* *Life events, etc.*	

Name	
Alternative Spellings	
Date and Place of Birth	
Date and Place of Marriage	
Date and Place of Death	
Parents	
Spouse	
Children	
Comments *Profession, Personality, Nationalities, Other spouses, Religion, Education, Siblings, Sponsors, Distinctive features, Languages spoken, Health conditions, Passport number, Life events, etc.*	

Name	
Alternative Spellings	
Date and Place of Birth	
Date and Place of Marriage	
Date and Place of Death	
Parents	
Spouse	
Children	
Comments *Profession, Personality, Nationalities, Other spouses, Religion, Education, Siblings, Sponsors, Distinctive features, Languages spoken, Health conditions, Passport number, Life events, etc.*	

Name	
Alternative Spellings	
Date and Place of Birth	
Date and Place of Marriage	
Date and Place of Death	
Parents	
Spouse	
Children	
Comments *Profession, Personality, Nationalities, Other spouses, Religion, Education, Siblings, Sponsors, Distinctive features, Languages spoken, Health conditions, Passport number, Life events, etc.*	

Name	
Alternative Spellings	
Date and Place of Birth	
Date and Place of Marriage	
Date and Place of Death	
Parents	
Spouse	
Children	
Comments *Profession, Personality, Nationalities, Other spouses, Religion, Education, Siblings, Sponsors, Distinctive features, Languages spoken, Health conditions, Passport number, Life events, etc.*	

Name	
Alternative Spellings	
Date and Place of Birth	
Date and Place of Marriage	
Date and Place of Death	
Parents	
Spouse	
Children	
Comments *Profession, Personality, Nationalities, Other spouses, Religion, Education, Siblings, Sponsors, Distinctive features, Languages spoken, Health conditions, Passport number, Life events, etc.*	

Name	
Alternative Spellings	
Date and Place of Birth	
Date and Place of Marriage	
Date and Place of Death	
Parents	
Spouse	
Children	
Comments *Profession, Personality, Nationalities, Other spouses, Religion, Education, Siblings, Sponsors, Distinctive features, Languages spoken, Health conditions, Passport number, Life events, etc.*	

Name	
Alternative Spellings	
Date and Place of Birth	
Date and Place of Marriage	
Date and Place of Death	
Parents	
Spouse	
Children	
Comments *Profession, Personality, Nationalities, Other spouses, Religion, Education, Siblings, Sponsors, Distinctive features, Languages spoken, Health conditions, Passport number, Life events, etc.*	

Name	
Alternative Spellings	
Date and Place of Birth	
Date and Place of Marriage	
Date and Place of Death	
Parents	
Spouse	
Children	
Comments *Profession,* *Personality,* *Nationalities,* *Other spouses,* *Religion,* *Education,* *Siblings, Sponsors,* *Distinctive* *features,* *Languages spoken,* *Health conditions,* *Passport number,* *Life events, etc.*	

Name	
Alternative Spellings	
Date and Place of Birth	
Date and Place of Marriage	
Date and Place of Death	
Parents	
Spouse	
Children	
Comments *Profession, Personality, Nationalities, Other spouses, Religion, Education, Siblings, Sponsors, Distinctive features, Languages spoken, Health conditions, Passport number, Life events, etc.*	

Name	
Alternative Spellings	
Date and Place of Birth	
Date and Place of Marriage	
Date and Place of Death	
Parents	
Spouse	
Children	
Comments *Profession, Personality, Nationalities, Other spouses, Religion, Education, Siblings, Sponsors, Distinctive features, Languages spoken, Health conditions, Passport number, Life events, etc.*	

Name	
Alternative Spellings	
Date and Place of Birth	
Date and Place of Marriage	
Date and Place of Death	
Parents	
Spouse	
Children	
Comments *Profession, Personality, Nationalities, Other spouses, Religion, Education, Siblings, Sponsors, Distinctive features, Languages spoken, Health conditions, Passport number, Life events, etc.*	

Name	
Alternative Spellings	
Date and Place of Birth	
Date and Place of Marriage	
Date and Place of Death	
Parents	
Spouse	
Children	
Comments *Profession, Personality, Nationalities, Other spouses, Religion, Education, Siblings, Sponsors, Distinctive features, Languages spoken, Health conditions, Passport number, Life events, etc.*	

Name	
Alternative Spellings	
Date and Place of Birth	
Date and Place of Marriage	
Date and Place of Death	
Parents	
Spouse	
Children	
Comments *Profession, Personality, Nationalities, Other spouses, Religion, Education, Siblings, Sponsors, Distinctive features, Languages spoken, Health conditions, Passport number, Life events, etc.*	

Name	
Alternative Spellings	
Date and Place of Birth	
Date and Place of Marriage	
Date and Place of Death	
Parents	
Spouse	
Children	
Comments *Profession,* *Personality,* *Nationalities,* *Other spouses,* *Religion,* *Education,* *Siblings, Sponsors,* *Distinctive* *features,* *Languages spoken,* *Health conditions,* *Passport number,* *Life events, etc.*	

Name	
Alternative Spellings	
Date and Place of Birth	
Date and Place of Marriage	
Date and Place of Death	
Parents	
Spouse	
Children	
Comments *Profession, Personality, Nationalities, Other spouses, Religion, Education, Siblings, Sponsors, Distinctive features, Languages spoken, Health conditions, Passport number, Life events, etc.*	

Name	
Alternative Spellings	
Date and Place of Birth	
Date and Place of Marriage	
Date and Place of Death	
Parents	
Spouse	
Children	
Comments *Profession, Personality, Nationalities, Other spouses, Religion, Education, Siblings, Sponsors, Distinctive features, Languages spoken, Health conditions, Passport number, Life events, etc.*	

Name	
Alternative Spellings	
Date and Place of Birth	
Date and Place of Marriage	
Date and Place of Death	
Parents	
Spouse	
Children	
Comments *Profession,* *Personality,* *Nationalities,* *Other spouses,* *Religion,* *Education,* *Siblings, Sponsors,* *Distinctive* *features,* *Languages spoken,* *Health conditions,* *Passport number,* *Life events, etc.*	

Name	
Alternative Spellings	
Date and Place of Birth	
Date and Place of Marriage	
Date and Place of Death	
Parents	
Spouse	
Children	
Comments *Profession, Personality, Nationalities, Other spouses, Religion, Education, Siblings, Sponsors, Distinctive features, Languages spoken, Health conditions, Passport number, Life events, etc.*	

Name	
Alternative Spellings	
Date and Place of Birth	
Date and Place of Marriage	
Date and Place of Death	
Parents	
Spouse	
Children	
Comments *Profession, Personality, Nationalities, Other spouses, Religion, Education, Siblings, Sponsors, Distinctive features, Languages spoken, Health conditions, Passport number, Life events, etc.*	

Name	
Alternative Spellings	
Date and Place of Birth	
Date and Place of Marriage	
Date and Place of Death	
Parents	
Spouse	
Children	
Comments *Profession, Personality, Nationalities, Other spouses, Religion, Education, Siblings, Sponsors, Distinctive features, Languages spoken, Health conditions, Passport number, Life events, etc.*	

Name	
Alternative Spellings	
Date and Place of Birth	
Date and Place of Marriage	
Date and Place of Death	
Parents	
Spouse	
Children	
Comments *Profession, Personality, Nationalities, Other spouses, Religion, Education, Siblings, Sponsors, Distinctive features, Languages spoken, Health conditions, Passport number, Life events, etc.*	

Name	
Alternative Spellings	
Date and Place of Birth	
Date and Place of Marriage	
Date and Place of Death	
Parents	
Spouse	
Children	
Comments *Profession, Personality, Nationalities, Other spouses, Religion, Education, Siblings, Sponsors, Distinctive features, Languages spoken, Health conditions, Passport number, Life events, etc.*	

Name	
Alternative Spellings	
Date and Place of Birth	
Date and Place of Marriage	
Date and Place of Death	
Parents	
Spouse	
Children	
Comments
Profession, Personality, Nationalities, Other spouses, Religion, Education, Siblings, Sponsors, Distinctive features, Languages spoken, Health conditions, Passport number, Life events, etc.	

Name	
Alternative Spellings	
Date and Place of Birth	
Date and Place of Marriage	
Date and Place of Death	
Parents	
Spouse	
Children	
Comments *Profession, Personality, Nationalities, Other spouses, Religion, Education, Siblings, Sponsors, Distinctive features, Languages spoken, Health conditions, Passport number, Life events, etc.*	

Name	
Alternative Spellings	
Date and Place of Birth	
Date and Place of Marriage	
Date and Place of Death	
Parents	
Spouse	
Children	
Comments *Profession,* *Personality,* *Nationalities,* *Other spouses,* *Religion,* *Education,* *Siblings, Sponsors,* *Distinctive* *features,* *Languages spoken,* *Health conditions,* *Passport number,* *Life events, etc.*	

Name	
Alternative Spellings	
Date and Place of Birth	
Date and Place of Marriage	
Date and Place of Death	
Parents	
Spouse	
Children	
Comments *Profession, Personality, Nationalities, Other spouses, Religion, Education, Siblings, Sponsors, Distinctive features, Languages spoken, Health conditions, Passport number, Life events, etc.*	

Name	
Alternative Spellings	
Date and Place of Birth	
Date and Place of Marriage	
Date and Place of Death	
Parents	
Spouse	
Children	
Comments *Profession,* *Personality,* *Nationalities,* *Other spouses,* *Religion,* *Education,* *Siblings, Sponsors,* *Distinctive* *features,* *Languages spoken,* *Health conditions,* *Passport number,* *Life events, etc.*	

Name	
Alternative Spellings	
Date and Place of Birth	
Date and Place of Marriage	
Date and Place of Death	
Parents	
Spouse	
Children	
Comments *Profession,* *Personality,* *Nationalities,* *Other spouses,* *Religion,* *Education,* *Siblings, Sponsors,* *Distinctive* *features,* *Languages spoken,* *Health conditions,* *Passport number,* *Life events, etc.*	

Name	
Alternative Spellings	
Date and Place of Birth	
Date and Place of Marriage	
Date and Place of Death	
Parents	
Spouse	
Children	
Comments *Profession, Personality, Nationalities, Other spouses, Religion, Education, Siblings, Sponsors, Distinctive features, Languages spoken, Health conditions, Passport number, Life events, etc.*	

Name	
Alternative Spellings	
Date and Place of Birth	
Date and Place of Marriage	
Date and Place of Death	
Parents	
Spouse	
Children	
Comments *Profession, Personality, Nationalities, Other spouses, Religion, Education, Siblings, Sponsors, Distinctive features, Languages spoken, Health conditions, Passport number, Life events, etc.*	

Name	
Alternative Spellings	
Date and Place of Birth	
Date and Place of Marriage	
Date and Place of Death	
Parents	
Spouse	
Children	
Comments *Profession,* *Personality,* *Nationalities,* *Other spouses,* *Religion,* *Education,* *Siblings, Sponsors,* *Distinctive* *features,* *Languages spoken,* *Health conditions,* *Passport number,* *Life events, etc.*	

To-Do List

Tips and Ideas
in case you are stuck in your research

Just starting out on your family research journey?

- Ask your relatives about their parents, grandparents and siblings. Try to get some names, dates and an idea of their life.

- Visit your local public office or archive and request your relatives' birth, marriage and death records. See what extra information is on them.

- Use free online family research websites and online national archives to look for your relatives. If you don't get a hit, try using alternative spellings, dates and locations.

Already have some experience?

- Look for your relatives using paid online genealogy platforms. In addition to getting further information on births, marriages and deaths, you might find your ancestor in census records, passenger lists, migration entry lists, military records or even in prison records.

- If you can't find your direct relatives in archives or on online platforms, look for people with the same or very similar surnames living at the same time in the immediate area. They may be cousins or at the very least, distantly related.

- Look for online public family trees that have some of your direct relatives or their cousins and spouses. You can find dates, names, locations and new spellings.

- Reach out to local archives with specific names and dates and ask them to confirm if your ancestors were born, married or died in that place. Be aware of the time and work that each search takes and keep on the archive worker's good side by not sending unspecified queries, lists with countless names or vague dates.

- If your relatives used to live in a small town reach out to the local city hall and ask them to forward your email to any living descendants.

- Try to interview the oldest members of your family. Don't limit yourself to just speaking to your direct relatives as their cousins, siblings' spouses and in-laws may know just as much. They might not remember names and dates, but you could get some good stories from them. You can then use these stories to create a timeline of your relative's life or to identify new names and places for research. You'll also be able to get a deeper sense of who your ancestor was.

- Consider taking a DNA test to find more potential locations of your ancestors. Make contact with DNA matches.

- Look at the back of old family photos and postcards. There might be relevant information about locations, names, dates or special events.

- Were your ancestors able to read and write? Find the local school of that time and ask for old student lists.

- Do you know what your ancestors used to do for a living? Were they public officers, doctors, teachers? Might they have been in the military or worked for an international company or a local shop that is still running? Reach out to that organization or to the educational institute they might have attended.

- Did your ancestors vote or have a passport or national ID? Contact your local authority and ask for their personal file.

- Get in touch with local cemeteries or look up online burial records.

Are you an advanced researcher with several years of experience?

• Try to locate the sponsors/witnesses that you have seen on your relative's records. If they are not alive, try to track down their siblings, sisters and brothers in law or children and interview them.

• Was your relative a member of any association, sports team or religious organization? Is that organization still running, even under a new name? Contact them and try to get in touch with old members.

• Has your relative written a book, article or dissertation? Check if it has a preface and who has written it. Try to locate that person or his/her descendants.

• Ask your older family members if they have funeral guest books. Track down people who are still alive or their children and ask for memories, photos or documents.

• Do you have access to online newspapers? Search for news about your ancestors.

• Visit your ancestors' graves and look for what is written on the grave. If it is a shared grave, take note of names and dates. If the cemetery is in a small town, look at the surnames on other graves. Their relatives might still be alive and living in the town.

- If your relatives have emigrated, track down other passengers that shared a cabin or class with them on that ship. They might have come together. Look for their children, nephews and nieces, and reach out to them. They could have old photos or documents about your relative.

- Google your relatives using special characters. For example, if you want to find relevant results and dismiss the noise, you should write your relative's name between inverted commas, add a word or year to orientate your search and a – symbol to eliminate irrelevant websites. Your search would look like this: "Michael Flannagan" Ireland -facebook -instagram -twitter

- Did your ancestors have land? Do you have old deeds? Use an online map, locate the current location of the property and visit the area. Interview neighbours.

- If your research should continue abroad and you can't travel, consider hiring a local researcher. The best way to start would be by reaching out to the local archive and asking for a referral.

Archive Log

Name			
Address / Website			
Phone		Date	
Email			
Contact Person		Role	
Records Checked			
Finds			
Next Steps			
Other Notes			

Name	
Address / Website	
Phone	Date
Email	
Contact Person	Role
Records Checked	
Finds	
Next Steps	
Other Notes	

Name	
Address / Website	
Phone	Date
Email	
Contact Person	Role
Records Checked	
Finds	
Next Steps	
Other Notes	

Name	
Address / Website	
Phone	Date
Email	
Contact Person	Role
Records Checked	
Finds	
Next Steps	
Other Notes	

Name	
Address / Website	
Phone	Date
Email	
Contact Person	Role
Records Checked	
Finds	
Next Steps	
Other Notes	

Name	
Address / Website	
Phone	Date
Email	
Contact Person	Role
Records Checked	
Finds	
Next Steps	
Other Notes	

Name	
Address / Website	
Phone	Date
Email	
Contact Person	Role
Records Checked	
Finds	
Next Steps	
Other Notes	

DNA Results Log

Name			
DNA Company		Date	

Ethnicity	Estimate %

Name	
DNA Company		Date	

Ethnicity	Estimate %

Stories to Remember

If you have found the Family Tree Notebook useful, please leave a comment on Amazon, as this will help to let others know about this genealogy tool.

If you have any suggestions or just want to say hi, you can reach me directly at
familytree.notebook@gmail.com

Thank you,
Juan

Printed in Great Britain
by Amazon